VOWED ECSTASY

NRITYANGANA KALA KENDRA

Copyright © Nrityangana Kala Kendra
All Rights Reserved.

This book has been published with all efforts taken to make the material error-free after the consent of the author. However, the author and the publisher do not assume and hereby disclaim any liability to any party for any loss, damage, or disruption caused by errors or omissions, whether such errors or omissions result from negligence, accident, or any other cause.

While every effort has been made to avoid any mistake or omission, this publication is being sold on the condition and understanding that neither the author nor the publishers or printers would be liable in any manner to any person by reason of any mistake or omission in this publication or for any action taken or omitted to be taken or advice rendered or accepted on the basis of this work. For any defect in printing or binding the publishers will be liable only to replace the defective copy by another copy of this work then available.

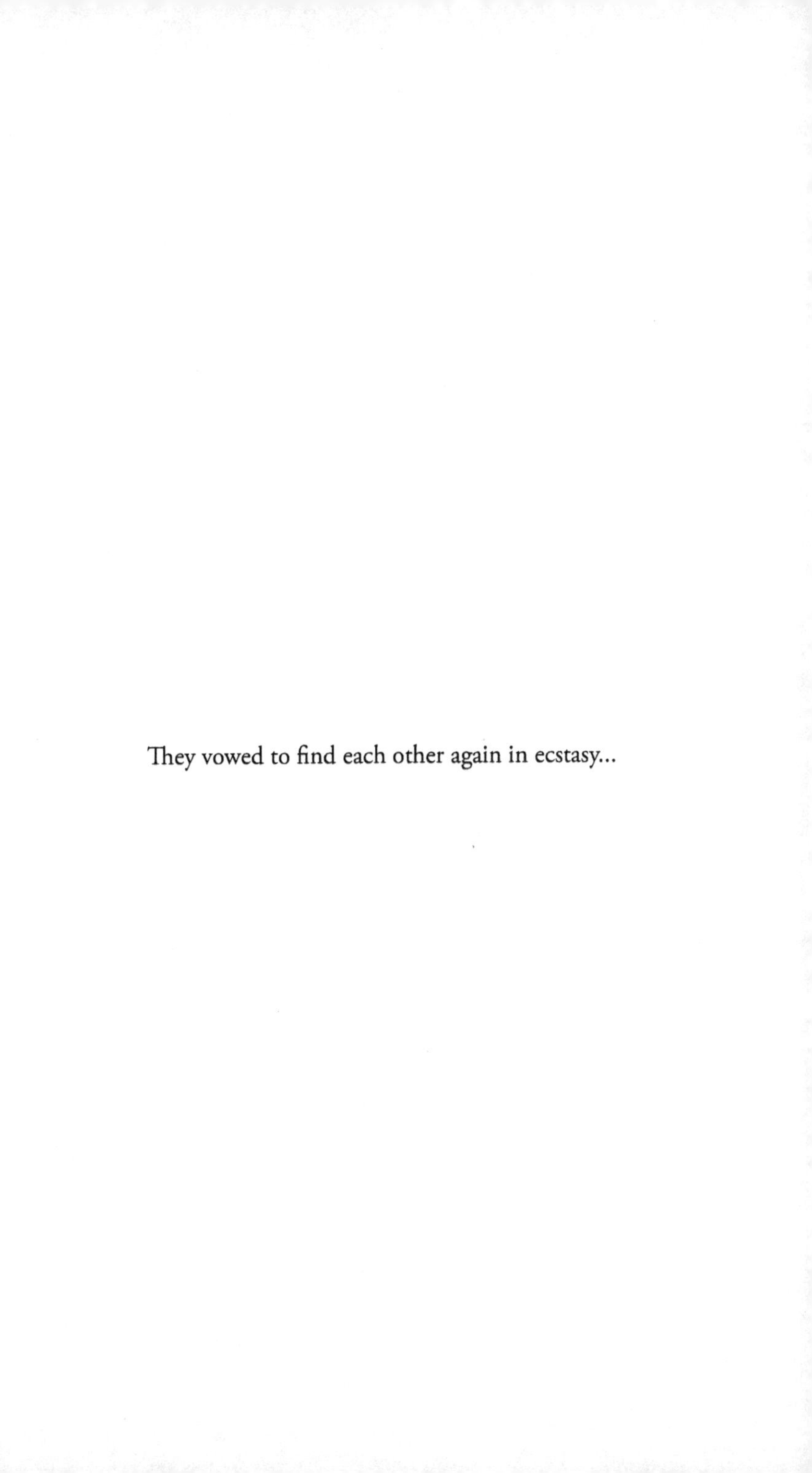

They vowed to find each other again in ecstasy...

Contents

Preface

"Vowed Ecstasy" is a collection of poetry that has shaped up via a poetry writing competition conducted by Nrityangana Kala Kendra. The beautiful submissions have been recorded here in the form of this anthology. The results and details have been shared in the book as well.

Acknowledgements

I'd like to express my deep appreciation and admiration to all the poets of this anthology. They have added value to this anthology just like how colors add gravity to a picture. The book wouldn't have been the same without their contribution. The project has been initiated by Nrityangana Kala Kendra OPC Private Limited. It was conducted via a poetry writing competition. All entries have been sincerely appreciated and gratefully acknowledged.

All the poems in this anthology are original pieces by our participants. No set of words can amount to my appreciation for them, namely - Aayushi Singh, Ananya Dutta, Chanchal, Dhruv Malpani, Dr. Neerja Deswal, Ritanwita Dasgupta, Sheetal Dubey, and Vaishali Bidhuri. The results have also been announced at the end of the book. I sincerely hope that the work presented in this collection is appreciated by the reader.

Nrityangana Kala Kendra

Nrityangana Kala Kendra (OPC) Private Limited is a company started by Miss Swarnika for the education of various art forms along with the promotion of extra-curricular activities. The company deals with research and exploration in the various forms of art as well. For different forms of dance, art and music, there are yearly certification programs that come with online examinations.

There are research groups along with performance troops organised from time to time. Language and literature are chiefly appreciated and endeavoured. The company collaborates and initiates ideas that are later compiled and published as books with the efforts of the team. The company also conducts competitions and functions for artists of all ages to showcase their talent and get felicitated for the same.

Nrityangana Kala Kendra was started to keep the classical roots of Bharatnatyam and Kathak alive, but with time the company broadened its horizon to encompass other art forms as well. The company also organizes skill-enhancement courses and workshops every now and then.

The online courses and programs have commenced. The company is registered with ISO 9001:2015. It is also accredited by IAF and EGAC.

Website- www.nrityanganakalakendra.com

Course Store- https://edu.nrityanganakalakendra.com/s/store

Email- swara@nrityanganakalakendra.com

Swarnika

Editor and Compiler

Swarnika is an avid reader and an ambivert. She is a glass-half-full kind of a person, not because she is always an optimist but because she believes that a glass that is full has no more scope and ends up creating the most amount of spills.

She completed her Bachelor's and Master's degree from the University of Delhi. She has completed her three-level professional certification in Spanish from Valencia Polytechnic University, Spain. She has also completed her certificate program in French from St. Stephen's College, University of Delhi. She is currently pursuing a Post-Graduate Diploma in Business Administration from Symbiosis Centre for Distance Learning, Pune. She is working on her thesis and research papers to earn her Ph.D. degree in English Literature. She is also pursuing Korean language certification program along with another in Social Work and criminal Justice System.

She has a keen interest in criminology and detective fiction. Writings that indulge mystery and rationale speak volumes to her. She has earned her TEFL and TESOL certificates as an English language teacher. She is also a certified dance teacher with specializations in Bharatnatyam, Kathak, and Contemporary. She is also certified in Classical Music and Fine Arts.

She exhibits abundant admiration for food and would call herself a foodie. She believes in living in the moment rather than giving the moment the opportunity to live through you without you even realizing it. She has started her company- Nrityangana Kala Kendra OPC Private Limited on her own. She has been tutoring kids along with mentoring graduate and postgraduate students in academic and creative writing.

On some days she is a dreamer while on others she is a realist. She firmly believes in humanism. Nature mesmerizes her.

She has initiated this project and has edited the book along with compiling it.

Vowed Ecstasy

As I stepped into the realm of fantasy,

I was vowed to be bruised by ecstasy.

I was vowed being taken by ecstasy;

I was vowed to be amused by ecstasy.

.

I dived into the ocean

But was pushed off back at the shore;

While walking by the beach,

A wave took me away.

.

I walked on the sand

Looking for dunes

As I reached the spot,

The wind blew it away.

I looked for flowers

And found myself at a funeral;

Beautiful people lain down to ground,

With dying flowers uprooted away.

I looked for rain

And found a town in drought;

The nearby city has been swept clean

as a flood drown it all away.

Still in the desert,

I looked for water.

Confused with mirages

From an oasis, I walked away.

.

I still am in the realm of fantasy,

I am still vowed to be bruised by ecstasy.

I am still vowed being taken by ecstasy;

I am still vowed to be amused by ecstasy.

Featured Poets

Aayushi Singh

Ananya Dutta

Chanchal

Dhruv Malpani

Dr. Neerja Deswal

Ritanwita Dasgupta

Sheetal Dubey

Vaishali Bidhuri

Aayushi Singh

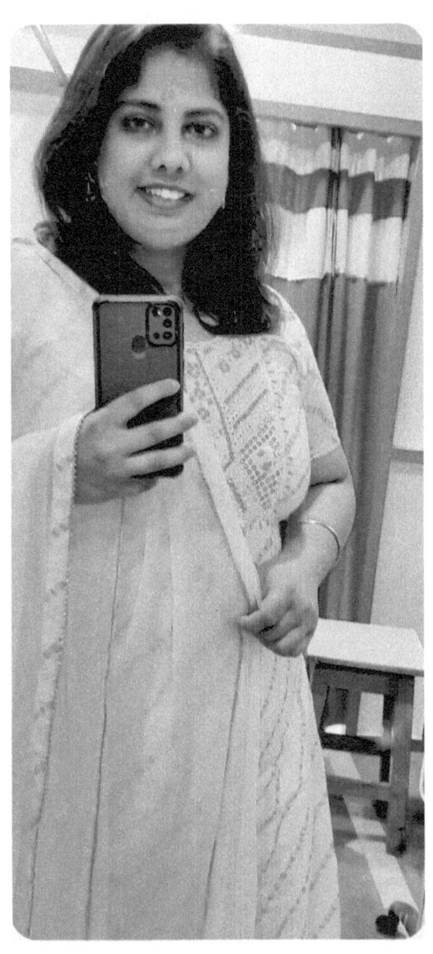

I am Aayushi Singh and I live in the small town of Chhattisgarh. I love to write and read and writing and reading is my relaxant. I am graduated. I feel like writing is a way to express your emotions.

It is all about having positive attitude and having a positive life with reality.

1. A Letter To The Loved One

Dear Loved One...

.

You know what beautiful things exist.....It is just inside you....never forget you are as beautiful as Nature. You just need to find it out and had to make it more attractive.

Never feel down just because others said you're bad. There is something best in you that makes you different from others.

Always it is not necessary that someone will be there to support you or encourage you all the time. Yeah sometimes you loss hope and sit at a place thinking you lost everything and you are good for nothing....but that is not 100% true.

Keep trying till you don't get what you want......

There are things which you have to do alone without expecting and complaining.....

So manage your own stuffs to make yourself better and play your role in efficient manner. Always remember darkness can be removed through light.

But.......

Living your whole life all alone is not possible and thinking that no one is really gonna help you out in your tough times is also wrong.....

So it is also true that somewhere someone is working hard for you and wishing to see you smiling. There is always a person in your life who is with you just to make you laugh and make you feel great. Someone is there who is fighting for you and love you more than you do. They do it with no complaints and no demands. Just they do it.

So never loose that person in any case because they are precious.

And always shine in a way you want.

.

.

From your well wisher......

Ananya Dutta

Ananya Dutta is an amateur who hails from a small town of the North Eastern state called Assam. English literature being her major discipline, she desires to excel in the field of literary composition someday. Furthermore, she is fond of the genre pop when melody is the matter, and fancies stars anytime.

The piece of composition was drafted on a the wave of a romantic feeling. By romantic, the indication is at the Romantic period in England which came to grasp form merely in the late eighteenth century and early nineteenth century, and hence the reference to William Wordsworth in the piece. The work intends to capture the attempt at the composer's eyes which beheld a strange sight during one of the hours of one early evening. With the pace of a to and fro motion, the composer descried the Mother Nature around the highest height she could reach, to speak of literally, but tried transcending merely in thought, with a special sight of her own red desk spectated right before letting the sensation settle in. This, the mention of her desk of 'morality' in the work. All and all, the piece of work strives to sketch a glimpse of whatever the eyes of the composer could capture during that early eventide.

2. On Nature

'Tis hard for me to tell thou what harkened my ears today and what beheld my eyne.

'Twas so out of my plan to witness, and I witnessed – something.

Art my hands cold, but dead; art they quite present on a young skin, yet merely appear wizened to me.

I saw them just in the moment back.

In this hour my fingers – index, thumb, middle, and little of the little one – all fiercely battle to write their own names on this pallid paper can they not touch through the tips the hath that spill these words anyway which may thy eyes read someday.

I saw my wrinkled hands, and scribbled three words, twisting the layers of the voile of the ventral plane of both my hands more and more, wetting the same with deep blue ink. I saw the skin twist, some lines contort right under the transparent blanket that sits atop all on both of my palms. Ah! And how they twisted!

The turn of every thin lining like yarn on the coat of my flesh, I saw it move, just slightly and no more. Why! It seems to move stealthily, so secretly it shakes like a scrawny lamb under my hungry watch.

And it went, composing careful curls –

One ramifying to many unprecedented branches.

My fingers – stalks of daffodils, not too slender, just there as extensions of a tree hath I not climbed as a child.

And there twisted the yarn of my skin again, weaving without a bodkin and wool, but creates it a delicate design.

But what is it today that mean I to tell? A second must I esteem for I know what to tell thee, but how to.

But thee see, was it something I saw with a mild desire, sweet vanilla in taste, of some drowsiness was that wet amidst the fog that surrounded me, my entire corpus, my legs and arms and back and front at the sixth hour of the evening today.

I saw the sun descend, slowly and slowly, reddening the cumuli, the nimbus and the stratus that hung as loads of water dying to fall in a wistful shower on the barren land of a farmer had whose stomach been a desert of its own for too long.

Wonder I how his lips must shiver in recitation of his holy utterance – a prayer he makes on the Angelus of the dawn, noon and dusk, wishing if only the bodies gravid with condensed vapors to burst open, and mother his soil.

Ah! How incessantly must it fall not in drops, not in sprinkles of thin jets of the water does my throat drown in everyday, but in a cascade, in aqueous masses of heavy clouds art that berserk with butterflies inside. Will they fall just like that thick white and foamy dew, only single in quantity, falls that from the leaf of camellia on a unit centimeter of the brown dry soil, the Earth encapsulated within that space in lieu.

Follow will the chains of a million such dews. Such was the welly of the clouds I saw. Ah! How heavy and filled to the bosom with white milk –

The fields – my fields, their fields were the infants crying.

'Twas light dark up in the sky. I walked as I sometimes do;

'Twas the same scenery in my neighborhood – street lights from a distance my sidereal stars through the foliage of the trees bore whose branches boughs of mango, peach, blue berries, gooseberry and pears in red, pink, blue and green. I should walk for some more time I pondered;

'Twere the mist, the creamy mist which smeared the lane from over the tree tops. I saw the unknown mountains from miles away. Art they still far from touch. Alas! Am I so grubby on their turquoise chastity. I am not a child anymore – this dirty dress my garb – what innocence I had merely one moment ago when I did not know.

Had the fog spread itself over their bonces too, was there a vapor trail across the treeline.

And walking a little more to and fro, hither and thither time to time, veering and in discipline all in tandem, I, oh my dear listener so patient so far, I the mere observer was crippled at the heart. Think I what if seek I no justice for this beauty? Will I let go of it, let go of it just like this? Why! Must I capture something in words.

A few feet away sat my desk in red plastic makeup, but alas! hath I lost my heart to it in this time.

Why! I attempted my tests of morality on it. So was I wrong to do so?

In the hours of desolation and dejection, in the hours past both noon and midnight, had it been my solitary scholar in need, had it been my consensual company. Should it not have happened?

That my table I personify, how shall I, if I may enquire, call thee a lifeless luxury?

How imbecilic, crass and bonkers must the others speak of me.

And here's the chart of my consensus to thee – there you have me, utterly mad, in love with everything now – tables, stools and the touch-me-nots that blossom beside the cesspool of my front yard.

But alack! How now about this beauteous zephyr on the skin of my uncovered legs and neck that is naked too for have I no scarf today?

What about this moment that I spend realizing how I am, on concrete cement do my feet scrape against the pebbles of? Am I alive now?

What doom must I incur, what hell betides my body if I, with hands that sway in mid air finding sheer nothing – but the breeze so unevenly thick and thin thwacking tangibly on my palms – swathe the skin is that covered in a red reefer jacket with this scene art my eyes blessed with sight to see, and my body clothed in a winding sheet of no color at all?

My pace has slowed down. I am walking slower and slower now.

I had come here looking for pain thou see. But was pain there in my inability.

What were all those particles in white cotton that flew about my visage, kissing yet hitting my face all the same?

Had I sought affliction with melancholy music, grey clouds swam above my head in an eclipse. Certain had I been, oh so certain to find it, but hark me right! Look how I digressed in the span of just blinks after blinks…

How were those bolts of strong knots finding my fingers? How? Must I know. Why! Did thee not think so?

Why! These restive and runic flaps of fireflies' wings all about my ears and eyes, how they entice and then tantalize.

Will I commit to wiles and ruses to have the corroded iron rod softly in my clasp.

Sits Wordsworth a few feet away from me in pages art that painted in sepia of a mild off-white hue – ten feet away from where my feet find room to stand, and I can tell that he is restless too.

Chanchal

I am Chanchal and I was born on 1 Dec 2001. I am pursuing English literature from Bharati college. I am a girl from a middle-class family in a village named VPOJharoda Kalan, Najafgarh(

New Delhi). I use my words in a way that is more intellectual but easy to understand by everyone.

Profeminist is one who supports feminist ideas and here in this poem, a profeminist is talking to her beloved that she was underestimating herself. By giving examples of other women who are forced because of others' thoughts about females, he is making her beloved know that her biggest enemy is her own negative thoughts about herself due to which she doesn't have self-belief. He makes her know how much power does the thoughts have? And how powerful is every female?

3. Profeminist

Mesmerizing dead lavender fragrance,
Make me think about you.
You were underestimating yourself.

.

I saw you locked in a cage.
Cage of your own thoughts about you.
And I saw you even getting embarrassed.
You think that I will hate but I didn't hate.

.

Think about a feminine,
Who is forcefully locked by others' thoughts,
And is made to lose hope.
At that time I will hate but not her.
Only the people who didn't help her to escape.

.

Because it's all about the thought we have made.
You should know you are a glass of red wine.
Beautiful and Divine.
You can stop every force.
You have the power to positively hope.

Dhruv Malpani

My name is Dhruv Malpani and I am pursuing Law to become a lawyer, but my passions include but are not limited to reading, writing, researching about space, literature, and history.

A brief and concise description of my poetry would be that it is about loneliness and how it deals with life and death.

4. Shackles

A helpless soul he was
Suffocated by the torments of the world.

.

Some things he said in words
But much in his heart remained unsaid.

.

Years of torture inculcated patience in him
But they also made him forget
What emotions were,

.

He saw himself as yet another drop of existence
In this vastness of the life ocean waters.

.

Fathoms deep down his soul
He was no more not dead
And there was no going back
He was sure.

.

He was alone
But it didn't bother him much before,
His loved ones had abandoned him
At least then, he had himself
But now, he lost himself too.

.

The world taught him;
Put on a happy face
But nobody cared to tell him
About the chaos that is being created within.

.

He would be so lost in his thoughts at times
That he'd even forget what he was reckoning about,
In the first place.

.

He gave up trying to break off from the chains
He had built for years now.

.

He was trapped in the walls
He designed ad infinitum.

.

He was enslaved by his own pessimistic musings
He was paused in his own imagination,
While the world moved forward with its innovation.

.

He locked himself in a completely lightless room,
Waiting to die,
To die, to dream yet again;
In his sleep of death.

.

He started laughing out loud
As his last few breaths drew away from him.

His laughter turned into cries of salvation,
And as his conscience grew,
He knew he didn't fear the arrival of death
He only feared the awakening into life.

But if he catered to that fear,
Then he would be no better than the rest of the world,

And thus, he decided to overcome that fear
And encounter it for the first time in his life.

So, he slowly stood up
Taking in the fresh air, breathing his first;
Undoing his act of entrapment,
Coming out of his imaginative world
Letting go of all the negativity.

And finally, started living for the first time
With a fresh perspective towards life.

Dr. Neerja Deswal

Neerja Deswal has been scribbling her poetic thoughts for many years. It was only during the pandemic, she found time and motivation to organize her notes and turn them into something more meaningful.

This poem is about the power of familial/filial love. Years ago, the female protagonist had moved away from her family after a bitter fight. But now, unavoidable circumstances have forced her to move back to her childhood home. She is afraid that she has lost the connection with her family. However, a gesture of affection by her older brother reassures her that they still share an unbreakable bond. This helps in reclaiming her life.

5. Lost and Found

As the rickshaw turns the corner of the street
I notice the bright yellow and red Diwali lights,
Cascading down the roof railing
Ending halfway in a knot.
Baba always ties them like that.
The mango tree, that we had planted after dadi passed away,
Looks bigger, older.
The house, I grew up in and once knew intimately,
Stares like a long-forgotten acquaintance.
I wonder if it remembers me.

.

I step inside hesitantly and ma envelops me in a warm embrace
Holding me a few seconds longer than usual.
I fight back tears. Pride forbids me
From letting her know that
I have come home broken and bruised by life.
But she knows. They both know.
Baba fusses over me,
Not asking directly but expecting to be told.
I awkwardly pretend to be tired
To avoid the lingering questions.

.

Next day, my siblings arrive with their families.
Soon, the ritual of catching up begins.
The cacophony thankfully drowns the awkward silences.
I curl up in the farthest chair unable to make a connection,
Silently absorbing the conversations.
Nobody makes eye contact with me.
At night, I sleep fitfully in my old room,
Surrounded by nephews and nieces,
Dozing between nightmares
Of past failures and future uncertainties.

.

When I had moved out after the bitter fight,
I had wanted to drift beyond a point of no return
And I could never go back.
With passing years, I assumed that they too had pulled
themselves away.
But today, here I am— leaning into my old life,
Like an unhinged door leans against the wall,
Hoping that they still care enough to catch me if I fall.

.

For the next few days, I find corners to stay invisible in.
Listening and not speaking.
Nodding and not drawing attention.
I imagine they resent me for coming back.
Sometimes, when everyone is busy,
I quietly wander in the rooms,
Trying to find the lost connection.

Once the festivities are over,
They all gradually depart to their busy lives.
My eldest brother is the last one to leave.
As the driver is loading luggage in the car,
We gather around to say the ceremonial goodbye.
Before leaving, Bhaiya gently ruffles my unkempt hair and smiles
'I hope to see you at New Year, Chhutki.'

In that one brief moment of affection,
I find what I thought I had lost forever,
And my life begins to heal.

Ritanwita Dasgupta

Well, I am a sensitive and exiguous person, not very coherent, but someone who is an epistemophile, loves to read and sing and play stringed instruments. Flawed but I seek perfection in my imperfections, kind of a people pleaser but also very tense, sometimes complicated, sometimes jolly. Just an 18-year-old thriving soul.

We all at times feel exhausted and that we are destined to suffer, that is because we don't treat ourselves with the same mindfulness as we take care of everything else except our own lustrous element, so to let that embark, this is a poem which acts as a reminder to love yourself as nothing in life is supposed to be synchronised and circumstances are not always in your purview.

6. Self Love

One of those components of life which are indispensable and help you exist,

Is that of your validation and self-realisation, to make you feel you have the whole world on your fist!

That opportunity to ruminate about what you expected from your little existence,

Of which it's hilarious to be recalcitrant and tense!

.

Perfection was never the key, we were born with fallacy and be saccharine,

But if you prioritize them over your self-estimation, you might never be able to get peace and time,

Nobody has subjected you to coercion, you are not alone conscientious to keep everything in place,

So go on our there and give your best, to intimidate yourself was never the case.

.

Just like you prioritize your ambitions like nurturing a plant or even your pet,

Do also give yourself the same love and care, as you deserve it, I bet!

Taking a break and maybe meditating or going on a detox spree doesn't render you inconsequential,

But it puts you actually, on a divine and spiritually high pedestal.

.

Your decisions and surroundings define you, so you know how to set the boundaries,
Do find pleasure in your own comfort zone as we all so rightfully need some respite as you're not supposed to melt in a foundry,
Do feel the desideratum to cry when you want to do so,
As penting up feeling will only accentuate the self loath, which you are not supposed to have also.

.

So go take that nap, cut yourself some slack, pour yourself that fat glass of wine
Think about your desires for life for a day, and let your manifestations intertwine,
Being aware of your strength and weaknesses to construct boundaries, was never a sin,
This doesn't render you inconsequential, but assists you to attain a higher spiritual self within.

.

When you're watchful of your own happiness, a more dignified version of yourself is already born,
Do not accuse yourself, or beat yourself up for being feeling things, you are allowed to feel torn,
Feel free to let go of gratuitously irritating people and, have trust in your own energy,

Seize the moment, inhale the essence of life, have fun and live with utmost dignity and vivacity.

.

You do have an esteem, and the potential to shine to your fullest,
So grow and evolve by setting your boundaries at its best,
Don't pay heed to what others have in store to think about you, as you are lustrous,
Allow yourself to make mistakes and learn, and from your own exuberance, don't be oblivious.

.

So go write that journal, vent it all out, go out with friends, take a break as you so deserve it queen,
Cook, sing, dance like nobody is watching, okay your instrument and do your thing, and to find peace be keen.
You are loved and cared and someone out there is rooting for you,
So do give yourself all the pampering you need and stay jolly, to add sparks in your environment too!

Sheetal Dubey

Born and raised in Mumbai Sheetal Dubey always had a passion for art and literature. She has completed her graduation in English Literature. To pursue her dream to become a teacher she's completing her post-graduation in Bachelor of Education. When she's not busy plotting the next story and poem in her head, you will find her reading stories from others. Lost in words that make much more sense than humans, she's an animal lover.

This poetry is about finding the courage to achieve one's dreams. It's about fighting the fears and taking that first step that will change everything forever. For reaching those goals that one has made in life. Becoming the strength that will encourage in achieving those goals and dreams. It's about accomplishing the unbelievable. Having faith in own self before taking that first step and living the life that they deserve without looking back or having any regret.

7. New Found Wings

With shining eyes,
She looked up at the white-blue sky,
Where she wanted to fly high.

.

The world has many heights,
She wanted to reach them all,
Despite the fright of her life.

.

She had a fear of heights,
Almost her entire life.
She darted into the air,
Saying Not today in her mind.

.

Without knowing the path,
She started to fly high,
With her newfound wings
On her cicatrix back.

.

Nobody could stop her now,
Because she got newfound courage to fly.

.

Her wings were shining brightly,
In the white-blue sky.

That was the sign,
She had flown,
And flown really high in this white-blue sky.

Vaishali Bidhuri

Vaishali Bidhuri has done Master's in English from Delhi University. she writes in English and Hindi-Urdu. She writes under the name of Vishi Wish. She loves to read poetry and watch movies. Her favourite colour is Sunset and her favourite word is Reverie. She believes that poetry is the most beautiful form of expression. Shades of life around her, inspire her to write. She currently writes for her Instagram audience. While constantly learning, she aspires to be a well-expressed poet and a writer. To know more about her writings visit her Instagram page <u>vishi0wish.</u>

The poem focuses on the state of mind where the mundane and everyday life gets boring and nothing seems to interest oneself.

8. No Solace

Sitting in my comfortable space
I can see the absurdity of it all.
A purposeless, homeless creature
Waiting for Godot.
The futile yet trying effort to make use of
Time-sickening endeavours!
The sudden urge to make sense of it,
Overwhelming revelation of knowledge,
And sinking profoundly into oblivion, silently.
.

I have seen the beauty of the mundane
Alas! the Sisyphus in me is irritated.
I need to change the boulder or the hill
I could even change the time of the labor.
Not just the mind but the body asks
A Change- before it turns to regrets.
I thought I think too much.
But no. It's the truth I haven't said enough.
.

My eyes are going to fall inside me
And silence will settle on the lips
It will happen soon. But I can change it.
Before it happens let me see and speak.

Why?? let me??!! Why do I still need permission?
It's the obedient child in me or the scared child
Seeking permission until the it falls apart.
Oh when love turns selfish and sprouts from fear
I know it produces a terrible terrible art.
When I look in the mirror sometimes
I recall that I once wrote I am an art.

Poetry Writing Competition

This book is the result of the successful completion of the
Poetry Writing Competition conducted by Nrityangana Kala

Kendra. We'd like to congratulate all the poets who have been featured in this collection. All of them are being awarded Certificates of Merit (electronic).

There were two outstanding poets who are being awarded for their exceptional work. Ananya Dutta bagged the first position in the competition for her beautiful poem "On Nature". Dr. Neerja Deswal attained the second position in this competition for her poem "Lost and Found". We heartily want to congratulate the winners.

First Position- Ananya Dutta (On Nature)

Second Position- Dr. Neerja Deswal (Lost and Found)

Thank You!

Dear Reader,

Thank you for reading this collection. We hope you enjoyed the pieces written by the poets of this book. In case of any feedback, feel free to write to swara@nrityanganakalakendra.com. We'll get back to you for sure. Your time is valued and we would appreciate your inputs.

Thanks and regards,

Swarnika

Director

Nrityangana Kala Kendra